AF223398

EDVARD GRIEG

PEER GYNT SUITES

No. 1 (Opus 46) · No. 2 (Opus 55)

Arranged for Piano Duet by the Composer

Bearbeitung für Klavier zu 4 Händen vom Komponisten

Edited by / Herausgegeben von

Adolf Ruthardt

EDITION PETERS

LEIPZIG · LONDON · NEW YORK

CONTENTS / INHALT / CONTENU

SUITE No. 1

Morning Mood

Morgenstimmung

Le matin

Edvard Grieg, Op. 46.

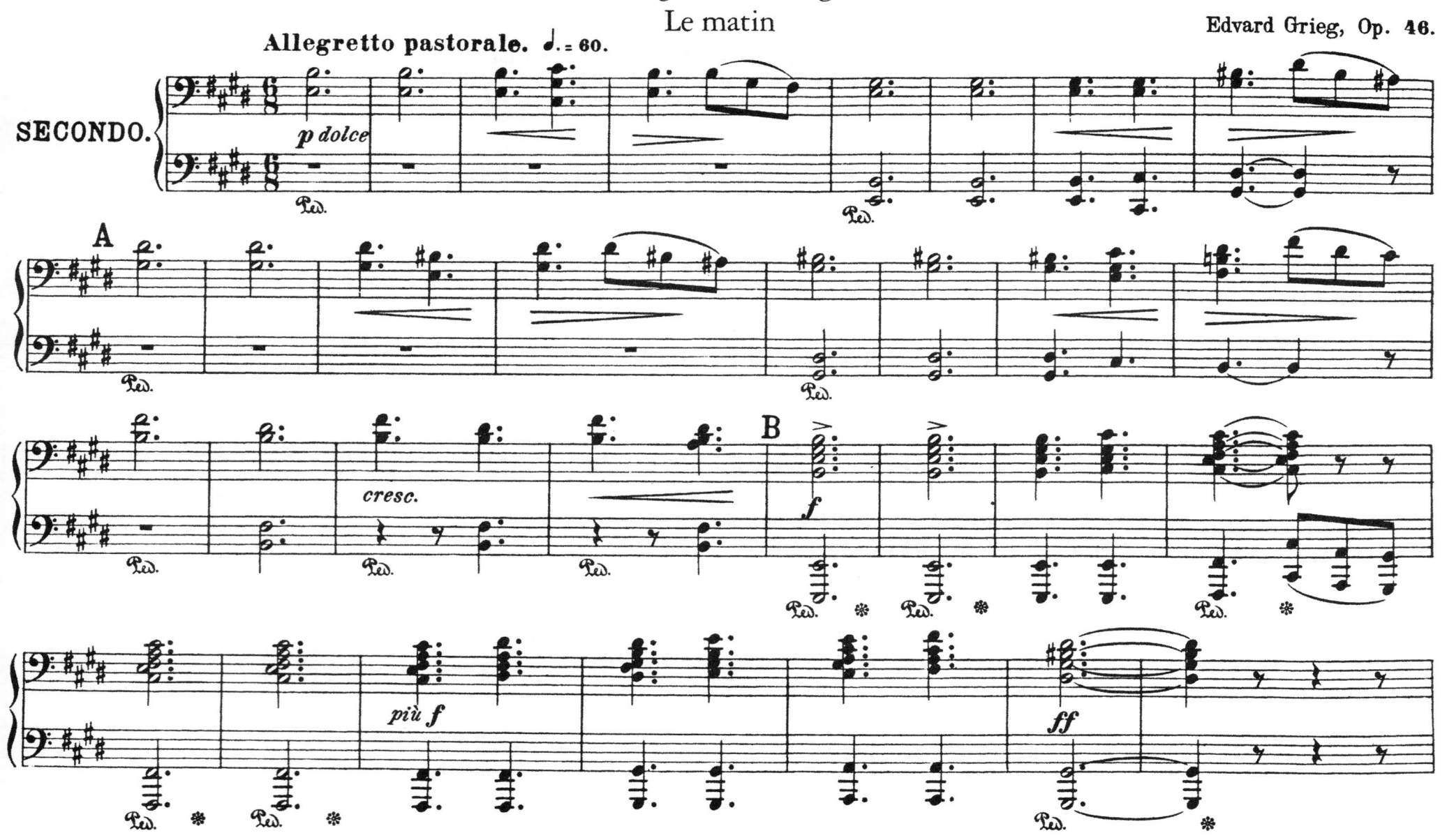

Edition Peters 7779

© 2005 by Peters Edition Ltd, London

SUITE No. 1

Morning Mood

Morgenstimmung

Le matin

Edvard Grieg, Op. 46.

Edition Peters 7779

The Death of Åse

Åses Tod

La mort d'Åse

The Death of Åse

Åses Tod

La mort d'Åse

Anitra's Dance

Anitra's Tanz
La danse d'Anitra

Anitra's Dance

Anitra's Tanz

La danse d'Anitra

+) Die Triller ohne Nachschlag.

In the Hall of the Mountain King

In der Halle des Bergkönigs

Dans la halle du roi de montagne

In the Hall of the Mountain King

In der Halle des Bergkönigs

Dans la halle du roi de montagne

SUITE No. 2
Ingrid's Lament
Ingrids Klage
La Plainte d'Ingrid

Edvard Grieg, Op. 55.

SUITE No. 2
Ingrid's Lament

Ingrids Klage

La Plainte d'Ingrid

Edvard Grieg, Op. 55.

Secondo

Arabian Dance

Arabischer Tanz

Danse arabe

Arabian Dance

Arabischer Tanz

Danse arabe

Peer Gynt's Homecoming

Peer Gynts Heimkehr

Repatriement de Peer Gynt

Peer Gynt's Homecoming

Peer Gynts Heimkehr

Repatriement de Peer Gynt

Solvejg's Song

Solvejgs Lied
Chanson de Solvejg

Solvejg's Song

Solvejgs Lied
Chanson de Solvejg